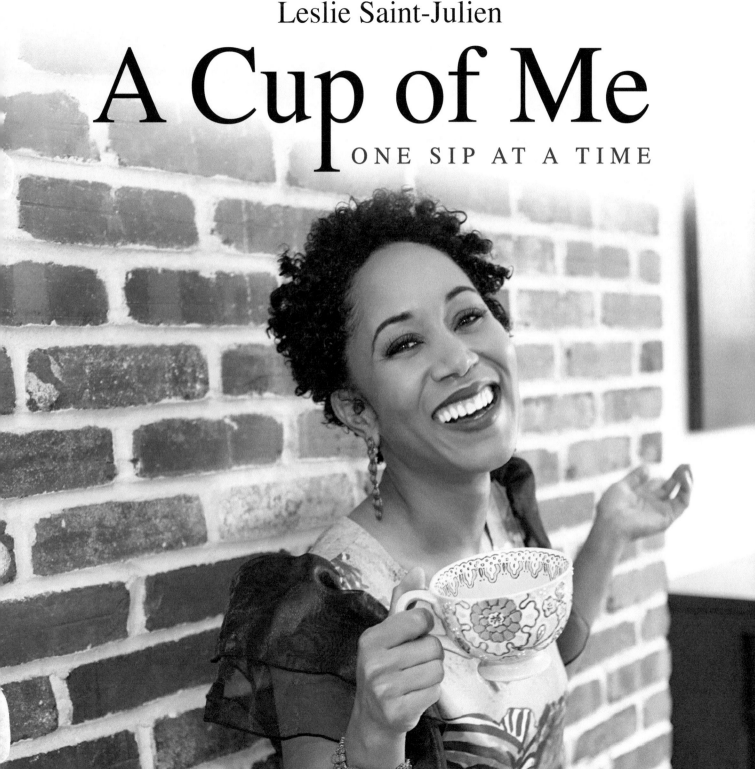

Leslie Saint-Julien

A Cup of Me

ONE SIP AT A TIME

AuthorHouse™
1663 Liberty Drive
Bloomington, IN 47403
www.authorhouse.com
Phone: 1 (833) 262-8899

Because of the dynamic nature of the Internet, any web addresses or links contained in this book may have changed
since publication and may no longer be valid. The views expressed in this work are solely those of the author and do
not necessarily reflect the views of the publisher, and the publisher hereby disclaims any responsibility for them.

Any people depicted in stock imagery provided by Getty Images are models,
and such images are being used for illustrative purposes only.
Certain stock imagery © Getty Images.

This book is printed on acid-free paper.

ISBN: 978-1-7283-6979-2 (sc)
ISBN: 978-1-7283-6980-8 (e)

Library of Congress Control Number: 2020915038

Print information available on the last page.

Published by AuthorHouse 08/22/2020

authorHOUSE®

Leslie Saint-Julien

A Cup of Me

ONE SIP AT A TIME

Sip slowly.

CONTENTS

Foreword 8

A Cup of Me 12

Afros Out..14

All Along 15

Joy and Peace...16

Unfailing Love...17

Be More 18

Adieu 19

Standing 20

Free Yourselves 21

Send Me..22

Truth, Light, Way..23

Dim 24

Rotten America..25

Who Are We?...26

Lived for Love..27

Whole 28

Living Water 30

Decisions Haiku 31

What is Love? 32

From Afar 33

Joy 34

Forgotten 36

Blessed 37

Energy 38

Silence 39

Poetry 41

Vision 42

Cried 43

Battle Wounds 44

B.P.G.L. 45

Happiness 47

I Choose Me 48

Haiku Time 49

Thank You...50

Yes! 51

Listening Skills...53

S.W.A.K. 54

Good Morning...55

Why I Love Him 56

Time 57

Non-Haiku 59

Dream Haiku...60

Purpose Haiku 61

Love Letter Haiku 62

Thankful 63

Dream...64

Game of Love...65

Live Life...66

A Love Haiku 67

He Is 68

Not the One...69

Here's a Haiku 71

Mine 72

If Today 73

Right Timing 74

Prayers 75

Saved 76

Onward 77

BK Love Haiku 78

Seeing Heart 79

Story Haiku 80

One Sip 81

FOREWORD

It was summer. We lived at the same apartment community. The usual grilling and chilling session was taking place at the outside patio. From a distance, I saw her laughing elegantly and dressed simply in shorts. By the way she carried herself; I knew I had found a best friend. I joined her table and introduced myself. The conversation was effortless. We spoke about God, love, business and so much more. From that moment on, we became thick as thieves. Leslie had all the qualities of a high-flying, glamorous celebrity—she told me that she is an actress and that she is an author too. Her drive for life matched mine. She embodied the superstar image with class, charisma, and most importantly, genuineness. Since day one, it felt like we had known each other for years. We had so much in common! Even our partners shared same names, lol! Leslie is good people and has so much love to give. Today, as I write this foreword to her captivating memoir of poetry, I share words that I always hoped—and in many ways knew; I would have the chance to write.

–Fortune Tanatsa Madyise

Black lives matter.

Dear Family,

Our brothers and sisters are dying. I raise my fist up. I put my foot down to fight against all the injustices that we continue to endure. I will not remain silent. I will speak out, I will vote, I will march, and I will fight. I will do all that I can to ensure our betterment, wellness and safety.

The murdering of our Black family must stop.

In solidarity,
Leslie

A CUP OF ME

It is filled with love.
It is filled with faith.
It is filled with hope.
My cup of me.

It is filled with joy.
It is filled with laughter.
It is filled with courage.
My cup of me.

It is served warm and never cold.
It is made sweet and never bitter.
It is bold and not weak.
This is my cup of me.

Add to it, some strength in tears
and add my dreams to seal the layers.
Of all the cups I dare to drink of,
only this one answers prayers.

It has a fight within its bite.
Its aroma cuts the stillness of any air.
In the base there is a root
that never dies despite despair.

I'll drink it now and more forever.
It is the cup that sets me free.

And only I can pour into it
for it is a cup of me.
I pour in Blackness.
I pour in pain.
And I can taste the bloody stains
every time my brother's murdered
and every time my sister's being slain.

For every mother that has cried,
For every child that has died.
I put her tears into my cup
Though I've never carried one inside.
For all the father's being taken,
crying sons who cannot breathe,
Cannot breathe and calling mama!
I'm being murdered by a knee!
When kneeling is a postured prayer,
in position of respect,
now a weapon used for death,
now a cardiac arrest.
Now my cup is over flowing.
No more room to add a drop.
Now a potion of despair.
Now diluted by the cops.

Make it stop!

13

AFROS OUT

It is said that time heals all wounds
and mends a broken heart.
So, if time ever stopped
we'd be broken spirits roaming around
having fallen apart. But what if?
What if?
What if?
What if time had stopped at the moment
before we were kidnapped from our land?
What if time had stopped before we
planted our feet on sinking sand?
What if time had stopped at the time
when we were already free?
We would never be called niggas
and Queens and Kings is all We'd know who to be
What if?
Well there is no time.
Time doesn't exist!
The moment is now!
What-chu gonna do with it?
Because time is up!
Afros out! And fists up!

ALL ALONG

And he had been there all along.
Waiting for the moment when I
would write songs of his beauty.
Pacing for the time to arrive when I
would say that He knew me.
And tell the world that
I know him so fondly.
He had been there all the while.
Standing with arms open wide
for me to fall into.
Praying for me to just give you
a piece of my story, now our story,
now His glory. He loves me!
Keeping no record of wrongs,
for he had been there all along.

Joy and Peace

Joy does cometh in the morning!
Let weeping endure a night of tears
that won't fall on deaf ears,
For our God hears these liquid prayers!
Tears that stain pillows,
mimicking the drops of rain
against my window pane.
Forming willows of new growth.
But for a moment, let the cries speak
and ask your Father to hold you
in his bosom and warm you with is love!
Let the tears cleanse your spirit
and release you from
whatever hurt that once was.
Let his hand hold yours
and lead you to new heights!
Forget the former things and
welcome this new life!
Don't you see what he is doing in you?
Making a way in the wilderness
and streams in the wasteland!
Trust his plan! Trust your heart!
Trust your spirit!
Trust his spirit in you!
Trust the way that he takes you,
For his plan for you is true!
Joy does cometh in the morning!
As promised is the sun to rise,
peace, will – be – thine!

Unfailing Love

Just look to God above,
and there you will find unfailing love.
A love with no boundaries,
unmerited and unchanging it is.
God is waiting for you to be totally his.
A love awaiting your warm embrace
to gift you with His perfect grace.

BE MORE

Let us give more to each other,
than our bodies desire to claim.
Making visible our spirits,
that will never behold shame.
Let His love be our compass
that masters our way.
Calculating footprints to follow
that have already been laid.
Let His peace always be our stillness,
reminding us He's great.
When in despair,
let us recall the master of our fate.
Let His joy be the filling,
of our drinking cup.
Quenching on the favor of
the blood dared given up.
Let His word be on our lips
to always lay upon our soul.
To be gentle and kind and from
the bosom of He who makes us whole.
And last, yet not least
Remember most to give God praise,
For what is now and what's to come,
forever and always!

Adieu

How do I embrace thee?
With all of my soul.
I let go, and let Him take total control.
How do I behold thee?
With spiritual lens.
Baring the truth
of a love without end.
With syncopated reflections
we may both draw
images of glory.
Telling our story.
The truth really is
a love without end.
Adieu, until we meet again.

Standing

I let the Holy Spirit in,
and blew the smoke out.
Casting out all doubt.
I let only love live inside of me.
I am free!
Praises to God daily I shall shout!
Ever since I decided to love him,
I have never experienced a love drought.
I was made for this!
His love in me conquers all!
I stand whole,
for with God at my side
I shall never fall!

Free Yourselves

How grateful I am to know thy face,
to know thy voice and feel your embrace.
How grateful I am to know thy name
and know I am your daughter!
To know the truth,
to know the way,
to now see clearly what was once a blur.
Visions turned into reality
as I drank up of your living water!
Running, I am, hurriedly to share
of your light and confess of your glory!
I must tell the stories
that might wake up the souls of the dead
who walk lost desiring to be fed,
and to be found!
I must sound!
Sound the alarm and ring it loudly!
It's time for everyone to know thee!
We are in dire need of saints
to paint the streets of this new Egypt!
We need freedom!
Saints, I say we need freedom!
But did you know that you can free yourselves?

Send Me

When I hear His words,
it never fails to pierce my soul.
it never fails that tears unfold.
When I think about the goodness
and the mercies that
He has granted me,
it is my duty that I touch souls
and set these words inside of me free!
I will go!
I will go, wherever God sends me!

TRUTH, LIGHT, WAY

We were born to live.
To live and be filled with
God's most perfect love,
then to die.
To die indeed,
will be the remnants
proving what was.
Proof that God renewed us,
and died away was the old us.
Proof of God's ability
to bring about change.
The lesson, dear loves,
is to learn the Truth,
to seek the Light,
and to learn the Way!

DIM

We were without sight,
operating under the moonlight.
Dim was the truth of our potential.
By the time the sun lit our path,
we had already taken the wrong steps.
Though, already stolen from each other
were our breaths.
Now I, speaking for myself,
decided to let my heart take the test.
I released my love in attempt
to salvage what was left.
Then I realized
there was no blueprint to begin with.
So, nothing could be saved.
Nothing could be made
of what never saw the day.
For, we were without sight,
operating under the moonlight.
Dim was the truth of our potential.
And even love,
didn't serve to be essential.

Rotten America

America has our blood on their hands,
still kissing our manifestation
that insists it's their story to tell.
Robbed from the anchorage of our
bosom causing fish to smell
as the death of us wash up on the shores
of hell!
Something is rotten in America!
It reeks of arrogance and self-interest!
Oh how did we get in this?
How many likes
do you see on my feed?
How many people are following me?
I love you! I'm angry!
I'm shedding a tear! Now, I'm streaming
live
so you don't have to be near!
America, perhaps you forgot how wide
He was stretched?!
How they whipped Him to the bone
and through the bloody flesh.
And even in the last
and final hour of His death,
he asked God to forgive them and give
his enemies breath.

Here we are in a country
that thrives on wealth beyond its need,
yet our brothers and sisters are dying
right beneath our feet.
We stand and watch us
time after time getting slayed. We sit
around and talk about it
for a few days.
We change our profile pics
to say, we're tired of it all and state
that no more Black lives need to fall,
hashing out our anger writing tags on
our walls! Taking to the streets, voicing
protests,
singing disapproval
of the state of affairs with unrest,
feelings of hopelessness rise
because it seems like
America doesn't care!
It seems like America doesn't care!
Well, let us core this apple that started
the sin.
America is rotten,
and it's rotten from within!

WHO ARE WE?

If He can make the birds to fly,
then He can surely make my spirit to sing.
Providing me with melodies
from heaven's mountaintops,
where I can hear "freedom ring!"
If He can lay His son to die,
then rise Him up again,
cleaning off our slate of sin
and forgiving us for them.
If He can love us nonetheless,
despite the foulness of our mouths,
speaking words that have no life
yet feed a sinner's doubt.
Then who are we to ever question,
who He is and how He dares?!
When in our hands we hold the power
to make deaf the sounding snares!
We can activate His grace
when we confess to our ways.
His love is undenying
as He made His son to pay.
Enabling his favor,
breaking bread at the table to pray,
we dare to gather as if a right!
We need to recognize this grand gesture
as a love that judges not,
in spite of our inability to love Him back!
Who are we?

LIVED FOR LOVE

In my reality where I did dwell,
I met many men I loved so well.
They said they loved me too,
and then they broke my heart.
I should have known it from the start.
They showered many other women
with their love and glee.
But, they told them things they never
told me.
Now, I know the reason why.
Those men and women
were so much weaker than I.
I ran all the way home,
and cried no more.
Not a word to my mother
as I walked through the door.
My father came home
late that night,
And heard my silence from left to right.
He entered my room

to check on my feelings,
And found me praying,
to God I was kneeling.
He closed my door
while nothing was said,
And then I wrote
this note to be read:

When God decides to send me home, Shed
not a tear, let out no moans.
So is my time, written for me.
Let God and I cry, sweet victory. Just dig
my grave, and dig it deep.
Place stone and marble, from head to feet.
Then on my grave implant a rose,
one that is blue, unlike what's known.
Unique it is and rare to see, there's only
one that echoes me.
Then from the head, release a dove
to show the world I lived for love.

WHOLE

If you will choose to run,
Then run, beloved,
towards the sun and towards the light.
Towards the thing that is bright.
Towards the energy that is right.
Towards the power that gives you sight.
If you will choose to run, beloved,
run away from yourself and be delivered.
So that when you love,
you can love with your whole heart,
and love with your whole soul.
God wants all of you.
Let him have total control.

LIVING WATER

Memories sometimes
fade as time has its way
and new beginnings
come to play in life's days.
Though, never should
the remembrance
of how we've arrived
escaped our minds.
Lest we be blind!
See Him in us!
Believe in this love!
You son, and you daughter!
Then out of your heart
will flow rivers of living water.

DECISIONS HAIKU

Give me a reason to stay
or wings to fly.
Touch me with hello's
or say goodbye.

What is Love?

Love is allowing silence
to speak when two hearts beat.
It's holding hands and kissing feet.
Love is thoughts without words
when four eyes meet.
It's seeing clear
what hearts do speak.
and if there are no eyes to stare,
love will tell you when it's there.
It is patient,
it is kind,
and most of all
love is divine.
It's yours to have
and yours to keep.
Love is you.
Love is me.

FROM AFAR

I want to be the touch you feel when we are apart.
Flowing through your body and running to your heart.
So no matter the distance, the day or the time,
I'll be in your presence, and you'll be in mine.
Embracing you with these words, If I may.
For my hands cannot touch
where you are today.

JOY

I have seen too many tomorrows
to cry over yesterdays.
I'm blessed to caress a new day.
Saved by grace and made with love,
in me lies the truth of an undimmable light.
Its torch is the son and faith be my might.
I shall never see the darkness of the day.
This lady doesn't sing the blues.
Melodies from heaven fill my womb.
Good morning, joy!
Thank you!

35

Forgotten

I really can't remember
your name.
Is that a shame?
Once upon a time,
I used to know you.
Memories of you
are slowly fading away.
Morning by morning,
I draw closer to the sanity
I always lived.
Leaving behind
the chaos that you fought to give.
No thanks brother,
I'm good.
I wish you would try to pull me
into your tragedies of false promises
and misunderstoods.
I fight with two hands.
That's why I wrote
your name in the sand.
So when the tides would come,
you'd wash away, understand?

Blessed

Tomorrow is now today.
Washed away are the
unkept promises of yesterday.
I call the morning good everyday.
There are no wrongs,
only rights
when the dawn meets you
with the gift of life.
For every breath you take is proof
you've made it through the night.
So here you are.
To live.
To breath.
To be.
The Lord keeps blessing you
and He sure keeps blessing me.

ENERGY

Naturally mystic vibes
sounding like wind chimes.
Spirits moving kinetically
as they traveled at the speed of
illuminating hearts.
This path set them apart,
from counterfeit dreams.
Reality took the driver's seat.
Truth lit the beams,
fueled with life!
This! Is seeing without sight!
Closed be my eyes,
remaining still as I might.
Letting this sun,
brightest of the bright,
light a sister's day
and be a brother to her night!

SILENCE

Silence.
This was the sound
that played in the darkness
of the night as she listened
for the sound of music that sounded
from the strings of her heart.
Silence.
The gift he gave her
that allows her to hear
when his presence is ever
so near.
Silence. When peace
became her new addiction
and all she could hear is God.

In memory of those who transitioned on to the next life during a time when God has called us to be still. To those who have survived COVID-19, God is till calling you to do His work.

POETRY

Music to my ears.
Silence to my fears.
Peace to my slumber.
Joy to my tears.
You.
Me.
Here.
Poetry for years.

VISION

If we had no mirrors
and no eyes to see,
how colorful
would our imagination be?

CRIED

I cried my last tear over you.
Leaving stains on a pillow that held
residue of your lies.
I cried.
Though, regaining control of my breathing,
exhaling relief that your
leaving was the best part of it all.
So, I cried my last tear.
Leaving stains on a pillow that held
whispers of your fears.
I cried and I cried joy,
in the morning!

BATTLE WOUNDS

Private moments shared.
New wounds needing repair.
Though the memories may fade,
the scars will still be there
to tell the story of how you cared.

B.P.G.L.

Balance,
what it means to have peace.
Peace,
what it means to trust God.
God,
what it means to love.
Love,
is breathing.

HAPPINESS

All I want to see
is that smile on your face.
That visual embrace
that erases my woes.
Allowing me to let God and let go.
Giving total control to love's hand.
Extending from the arm of a real man.
All I want to see is your smile.
Thanking God for the while
that was worth waiting for.

I Choose Me

If it's not me you desire
then let my freedom ring!
Let me keep climbing to the mountaintop
so you can later look up
at my next higher level stops.
I'm not here to play games.
It's a shame that you don't
know the way to my heart
by now for as long as you've known my name.
Your GPS should have
told you that you have arrived.
But these new roads unfamiliar
to your navigation has you
feeling uncertain inside.
You're examining the time
it has calculated for you
to reach this destination.
All this lacking of trust,
is catastrophically
tearing you away from us.
So just go if you must.
And save me the little time
I have left.
Don't rip my heart from out of my chest.
Please leave me with
at least my breath.
For my Father says
my business is life,
not death.

Haiku Time

Time waits for no one.
Put your foot to the pedal.
Take no passengers.

THANK YOU

Thank you for being true.
Thank you for the joy
That is new,
ever so peaking through
a blue morning's dew.
Thank you for the first time
of the beginning of forever
with you!

YES!

Ask me if I would live it again,
this thing called life.
Only if it lands me in your arms
at that moment
when you took my breath away.
Again, I would navigate
through the labyrinth
of my journey to you.
Again, I would endure the pains & the joys
that make everything now so beautifully true.
Again and again, I would test my faith allowing
for the bumps and bruises
and the mistakes.
Again, I would allow for tears
of strength to fall where they may.
After all, I'm stronger today.
Because of this life,
I am blessed!
So ask me today,
if I would live it
all over again?
Unequivocally yes!

Listening Skills

When God says yes,
then, obey Him and go.
Don't listen to the haters
or to the voice that says no.
When God says yes,
then, child, believe!
No need to discuss it,
just let the thing be.
When God says yes,
know that you are safe.
And know that he'll guide you
and time will not waste.
When God says yes
Say yes too!
Show him your gratitude
by saying thank you!
But when God says no,
just know it's for the best!
For if He wants it for you,
He will simply say yes!

S.W.A.K.

Two hearts awoken
by the sound of love's chime!
One language being spoken!
Open minds,
to tomorrow's ways,
trusting their alignment
from their yesterdays!
God played this hand,
no one needs to understand!
Trusting His plan
is all that matters!
We flatter Him,
with obedience
and benevolent consistency!
He sets us free!
Allowing us the opportunity
to either strengthen
or shatter our fate!
I prefer not to infuse the latter.
With a kiss, we can formerly
seal this first date.

Good Morning

Might you be
the sun rays of morning
that I speak of in my drawings of words?
A wind blowing kiss reminiscent of
the first time we wished for our songs to be heard!
And, sing did we much! No limit of
the time made for us!
Intertwined like paint to a brush!
Passion met love without lust!
With you
my heart I entrust!
Might you be
the sun rays of morning that
I speak of in my drawings of words?

WHY I LOVE HIM

I will begin by thanking God
for placing you in my view.
I had seen you before,
but on this day,
my vision was new.
Who knew?
What was forming was taking its time.
Unfathomed possibilities took their
own path to find.
He's been kind.
Preparing and lighting your way.
I, having had lessons
that prepared me for today.
I am ready to confess
how I want to love you
and take our next steps.
No regrets.
I am grateful I moved.

Surrendered it all
so that I might be used.
Then you came.
Mirroring a parity of gifts.
Speaking in a tongue
that caused my spirit to lift
and to shift!
I had felt this before.
Though immature was my spirit
at the time to crave more.
Now I've grown.
With new vision I see
how you look at all of the beauty
that breathes within me!
And I know,
for I too see within,
what's beautiful in you is
why I love Him.

TIME

If time had stopped before I could
breathe all my words to thine,
a love like yours
would never touch
this pulsating heart of mine.
If time had stopped
when I did part
my lips to twine with yours,
the taste of goodness
I would know never
sipping blandness evermore.
If time had stopped
at the morning's wake,
where you met me with your eyes.
Unwritten would these words
be painted in the blueness of the sky:

To you, from Me.
A gift she is.
Be sure to love her carefully.
I trust her hands to love you too,
as I have touched them personally.
So be in love, be in Me,
most of all,
forget me not.
For all her love
you would not know
if time had ever stopped.

58

NON-HAIKU

Without eyes to see,
He calls me beautiful.
Now that's love.

DREAM HAIKU

That feeling that stays.
You still feel it in your sleep.
Life of a dreamer.

Purpose Haiku

The freedom to smile!
Doing what you truly love!
Purpose driven life!

LOVE LETTER HAIKU

Dear daughter, don't fret.
I already paid the cost.
Love letter from God.

THANKFUL

And when the morning came to so arrive,
where newness had begun,
I looked at your delivery of another warming sun.
I saw the hairs upon my skin
and felt the brittle of your breath,
reminding me of these two gifts
when I have nothing left.
In times we may feel hopeless
as we meddle with our course,
but what's important to remember
is that we're built to ride this horse.
What God has planned,
is not for us to question or to doubt.
Our job is simply to remain
in faith and trust the route.
So with the brightness of the moon
it marks you've made it through.
Be thankful always for the night
as the morning touches you.

DREAM

Be a dreamer.
Be a thinker.
Be a hoper and believer.
Be the vision that you see,
Be the one to make it clearer.
Be alive.
Be awake.
Be unafraid to make mistakes.
Be determined.
Be committed.
Be the now and not the waited.
Be the author of your life.
Write your visions to be seen.
Never dare to sleep.
Only dare to dream!

GAME OF LOVE

Combing through my pain
I wasn't in the mental space
to hear his name.
But ever since I let him in,
my sadness has been on a train to yesterday.
And only joy, pure joy
is riding in on the morning train.
The arrival of this time.
As perfect as it is, I could never,
and will never utter his name the same.
Now that I could see
my beautiful tomorrow
standing right in front of me.
I know that love
is the name of this game.

LIVE LIFE

Dreamers seek dreamers!
Lovers of life are
earth walking healers
bringing medicine
to the souls of the wounded hearted
who's spirits have departed
and fallen silent to deaf ears.
Let's be clear,
dreamers are believers
of what's real.
They understand how to taste,
touch and feel.
This life is to be lived.
If not lived then why be?
So keep dreaming, beloved!
If not for thee, dream for me!

A Love Haiku

Feeling butterflies.
Floating on cloud number nine.
When falling in love.

HE IS

He is magnificent.
He inspires me.
He's in love with me.
He is marvelous.
He is mine. (And I am HIS)
He is more than me.
He is maker.
He is mother.
He is mover.
He is mild.
He's indescribably magical.
He is me.
He is morning!
He is music to my soul.

Not the One

He spilled milk.
I didn't cry.
I could care less about the bottle
being drained of the sour
that poured out of his mouth.
Furthermore,
it was the core that stung.
When he unleashed with his tongue
words that can never be unsung.
A feeling that could never be undone.
As I sit and recall recorded memories,
it might plain me to see he was never the one.

70

HERE'S A HAIKU

I call it a gift.
Some might call you to be blessed.
Either one, I'm here.

Mine

I have a reason to cry!
Cry as I may
to the penetrative sound of music that
your heart plays as we lay.
Hearing an array of
stringed chords being played
causing eyes to water
from real love being made.
I'm captivated.
Long awaited.
I'm receptive to your loving ways.
In anticipation of our future days that do lye.
When I will say with conviction
there's a You and an I.
I'll have a reason to cry!
Shouting praises
to the Heavenly skies!
Thanking God for the ride
to this time of His
making you
unequivocally mine!

IF TODAY

If today is your morning,
then rise up to the dawning
and follow the blueprint
of the drawing for your life,
God's map already drawn for you,
if today is your morning.

If today is your morning
and you can see the sun,
then embrace the rays
of this day giving thanks
for a part in this play
called life.
If today is your morning,
live!

Right Timing

It's different this time.
Specifically the atmosphere
has me seeing more clear
what had been in my view
for so many years.
It wasn't until now though,
until this time
that I could behold
the truth of the matter
that had already been told
to my spirit.
I'm in this.
We're in this.
Because He did this.
How so?
Well, we glow!
You've always been mine.
And so divine was His whisper
to thine own ears
saying, it's time!

PRAYERS

She's more than you see.
Have you ever heard tears speak?
Poured liquid prayers.

SAVED

Staring into the mirror
I see the vision
that once played in the mind
of my younger days
when nothing but innocence
tugged at the war of my ways.
I remember how deeply I sought
His face.
I remember how much I wanted
to feel His embrace.
And so, I just asked:

"Come into my heart. Into that space,
where only pure love lives and never to leave me
so that you are all I have to give."

ONWARD

Though his lips bled,
his words were not read.
Instead,
I heard the pleading sounds of a man
troubled by where his heart has been led.
Not realizing that his actions did speak,
he told me all I needed
where words could not reach.
So in translation,
I'll deliver my response just the same.
Silent, be the morning
and forgotten be your name.

BK Love Haiku

Thoughts playing tennis.
The moon chased the sun away.
No sleep 'till Brooklyn.

Seeing Heart

You can choose to be open.
You can choose to be closed.
What really matters is your heart
which only God knows.
But behold are your eyes
which I can deeply see through.
And its windows are revealing
what I truly mean to you.
Is this love, is this love,
is-this-love-that I'm feeling?

Story Haiku

You must turn the page.
Otherwise you're not living.
What is your story?

ONE SIP

I'm here to interrupt
your programming.
We seem to have
gotten off course.
Final was this divorce the day
that you decided to rip us
from the bosom of
our motherland.
Though, technically
we were never
married to the idea
of joining this Union.
It only took one sip to realize that
you put poison in our cup.

And so we began our plan.
With our soldiers on the inside,
we learned a new language
then fucked what you heard.
Pardon my French,
Kreyol became the new word.
And getting our freedom back
became the new mission.
Then carefully,
we started mapping
out our positions.
Our tongues became our guns,

because we spoke freedom's
language. No army of Napoleon
could ever take us down.
From Senegambia,
to Jamaica we inherited
our crowns.

Thanks to Boukman
for cooking the pot.
Toussaint then led the first Black
Revolution to the mountaintop!
He opened the door.
And then, it got mean,
the Father took over,
Jean-Jacques Dessalines.
Without fear,
we had to slaughter.
It was payback time for the rapes
of our sons and daughters.
Mother Haiti we love you,
we owed it to you to set you free!
1804 on the 1st of January.
We took over that battleship.
And it only took one sip.
And so here I live, with
this blood in my veins my
parents carrying the stains

I'm feeling the pain.
Shit is not the same for me.
I'm wearing both sides
of the shirt see.
Brooklyn made me,
Haitians raised me
My Blackness is permanent
Can't nobody change me!
I got this fire in my chest.
Forever there will be smoke
in my lungs.
I can't be watered down because
that's just not how I was built
or where I am from!
I know who I am.
The question is,
do you know you?
Brothers and sisters
do you understand how
deep your blood runs?
We're not shook ones!
We're warriors!
Put your fists up!
Don't fall for the tricks!
And whatever you do
when that cup comes around,
don't ever take one sip.

But Jesus answered and said, Ye know not what ye ask. Are ye able to drink of the cup that I shall drink of, and to be baptized with the baptism that I am baptized with? They say unto him, We are able.

-Matthew 20:22 *(KJV)*

Acknowledgements

I would like to thank, God for helping me bring this book to life! Every word you have read came straight from the Most High and onto these pages!

Now for the heavy, I am delivering this collection to you during a huge universal shift. It's 2020 and the world is under attack. A pandemic has hit us and people all over the world are dying from the Coronavirus Disease (COVID-19). We have been living under quarantine for over 120 days. In addition, members of the Black community and family are being hunted, murdered and lynched due to unending racism. This pandemic and the murdering of Black lives has stirred much emotion and fear that has brought the entire world under fire. I pray that we will arrive to betterment, peace and wellness soon.

I could not complete the full packaging of what you hold in your hands without the support, love, encouragement, vision and care from my dear friends below. Thank you for everything!

Ananie Momplaisir, C'est Momplaisir Events
www.momplaisirevents.com, Instagram: @cmpevents

Ricardo C. Sandy, RCS Images
www.rcsimages.com, Instagram: @rcsimages

LyneLuvDance™, Instagram: @lyneluvdance

A very special thank you to the team of magicians who helped
to capture everything you see visually in this book!

Cover-to-Cover Exterior Design and Graphics: Ian Walcott, IanDesigns
Instagram: @iandesigns

Photography:
David Walcott II, SAG-AFTRA Point, and Shoot Pix
Instagram: @pointandshootpix @mr.walcottii

Makeup Artist: Manouchka Milliance, www.manniefique.com, Instagram: @manniefique
Face Mask Designed by Nellz, Instagram: @wrappedbynellz

inted in the United States
y Bookmasters